DAILY AT HIS TABLE

Harrison House

Shippensburg, PA

Harrison House Books by Patsy Cameneti

The Spirit Realm:
The Place We Work with God in Prayer

The Official Workbook for The Spirit Realm

The Official Summary of The Spirit Realm

Engendered: What Was God Thinking?
Gender Roles & Relationships

DAILY AT HIS TABLE

A 31-Day Devotional *for* Sacred Communion

PATSY CAMENETI

All emphasis within Scripture quotations is the author's own.

Published by Harrison House Publishers
Shippensburg, PA 17257

ISBN 13 HC: 978-1-6675-1263-1

ISBN 13 eBook: 978-1-6675-1264-8

For Worldwide Distribution, Printed in the U.S.A.

1 2 3 4 5 6 7 8 / 30 29 28 27 26

CONTENTS

IN LOVING TRIBUTE TO MY WIFE—PATSY CAMENETI

Even though Patsy isn't here to see her work published, I have a deep sense of joy and gratitude to God for His faithfulness. During our time together—both in life and in serving others—I saw how deeply her relationship with her Savior inspired so many others to seek a living and vibrant walk with Jesus for themselves.

Patsy was so determined to finish this book, not for herself, but because she truly believed it would help others find a closer connection with Jesus just as she did—every day. She hoped anyone who reads this book would discover Communion to be more than just a religious ritual, but a chance to meet a living Savior and experience His love personally.

In each daily entry, her revelation of Jesus' sacrifice is profound. Her love and appreciation of her Savior is alive on every page. Her voice and her gifting continue to speak through this book long after her earthly words have fallen silent.

Along with everyone who helped bring this book about, I want to celebrate Patsy's life and legacy. I hope that as you read you find a little bit of her legacy for yourself and that your walk with God grows deeper in the days and years ahead.

Tony Cameneti
September 2025

SETTING THE TABLE FOR COMMUNION

KNOWING HIM

A special meal calls for an appropriate table setting to highlight what is being served. Wouldn't it be unthinkable that a Thanksgiving or other special prepared meal be eaten on cardboard, scooped up with sticks?

I want to share some things for the purpose of setting the table for the most costly and precious meal of all. Communion.

The following scriptures, written by Paul in the later part of his life, provide a good place to begin.

> *Yes, furthermore, I count everything as loss compared to the possession of the priceless privilege (the overwhelming preciousness, the surpassing worth, and supreme advantage)* ***of knowing Christ Jesus my Lord and of progressively becoming more deeply***

> ***and intimately acquainted with Him*** *[of perceiving and recognizing and understanding Him more fully and clearly]....*
>
> *[For my determined purpose is]* ***that I may know Him*** *[that I may progressively become more deeply and intimately acquainted with Him, perceiving and recognizing and understanding the wonders of His Person more strongly and more clearly],*
>
> *...and that I may so* ***share His sufferings*** *as to be continually transformed [in spirit into His likeness even] to His death, [in the hope]* (Philippians 3:8,10 AMPC).

I was 19 years old when these two verses became the cry of my heart and theme of my prayers day after day. God gave a simple song that earmarked those days of spiritual hunger in 1977, declaring my reason for living was to know Him.

The delight of knowing Jesus and the desire to know Him more has motivated me over the years to study, pray, and walk with Him. A most precious way He gave me to draw near to Him for a season was through fellowshipping with Him daily with respect to His sufferings. I would do this while taking Communion in my home. I suppose I have taken Communion hundreds of times over the course of my life. But slowing down to fellowship with the Lord, allowing Him to teach me each day about Himself, was something different. More intimate. Holy.

As I would take time to prayerfully hold the bread and the cup, sometimes for a long period of time, He opened my heart to see and know Him more as He showed me more about the role of His body and His blood in the Father's plan to redeem mankind. As I became more aware of Jesus' body and blood, the more overwhelmed I was with the wisdom of God expressed through that plan to redeem fallen mankind. That season of daily communion with Him affected me profoundly and was the inspiration for this devotional.

One of the benefits listed as part of the New Covenant that Jesus' blood confirmed is that all would know Him. From the least to the greatest! To me that means that knowing Jesus intimately isn't meant to be exclusively experienced by only a special group of high-ranking ministers. No, it is a most precious benefit that everyone is to have—the experience of personally knowing the One who saved us! (Hebrews 8:6-13 NLT)

IT IS HOLY

My dad pastored the church I grew up in. I remember that we had Communion once a month, generally on Sunday morning. On occasion, we had Communion on Sunday night, as was the case on this particular night. We were served Communion as we knelt at the altar and were encouraged to take time to "commune" with the Lord.

I was probably around 11 years old at the time and got to chatting and laughing with one of my friends while others around us attempted to not be distracted by us. My dad tapped me on the shoulder and said that we would talk at home. I instinctively knew that this would be more than a talk and for sure it was. I believe it was my second to last spanking, and I've never forgotten it.

Before the spanking, Daddy explained why he was going to discipline me. He talked about how important Communion was. How sacred. And that the way I was behaving during Communion showed a lack of understanding, which resulted in disrespect for what Jesus did. I could tell Communion meant a great deal to Daddy. I remember that he cried when he was talking to me, and I wished he would just get on to the spanking part.

Well, needless to say, he taught me an important lesson of respect for this ordinance of the church; it was a lesson that immediately changed the way I acted during communion but was just the beginning of all the Lord would show me on the subject.

IT'S AN ORDINANCE

What's an ordinance? Water baptism and the Lord's Supper, also known as Communion, are two ordinances, or sacred practices that followers of Jesus are instructed to do. (Matthew 26:26-27 NLT; Acts 2:38 NLT)

It is through the ordinance of water baptism that we acknowledge and identify with Jesus' *burial and His mighty resurrection.* To understand resurrection power that is toward us who believe was something Paul prayed not only for himself in Philippians 3:10 but also for the entire church as we see in Ephesians 1:19 (NLT).

As glorious as baptism that depicts resurrection is, for this devotional, we focus only on the body and blood of Jesus before He was raised by the glory of God. It is in Communion that Paul says the *Lord's death* was proclaimed until He returns. (1 Corinthians 11:26 NLT)

While *communion* is the word commonly used for this sacred ordinance of receiving the bread and cup that represents the body and blood of the Lord, communion also has an additional definition: sociation; fellowship; interchange or sharing of thoughts or emotions; intimate communication.

The ordinance of Communion includes both aspects of the word. Communion through intimate fellowship with the Lord is to be part of the Lord's Supper to keep this very precious practice from becoming a stale, lifeless, religious act.

In every Gospel—Matthew, Mark, Luke, John—Communion is a practice that Jesus gave clear-cut direction to do. Paul quotes Jesus regarding Communion and added special instructions as well. Paul says that in taking the Lord's Supper, we proclaim *Jesus' death* till He comes again. (1 Corinthians 11:26 NLT)

And yet after all this attention, it can still have little influence in our lives. How can that be? Anything that isn't really understood can lose value, slip into routine, and have little to no impact. Some take Communion but don't really know why and wouldn't miss it if it wasn't offered. Others take it with their whole heart but still have limited understanding. For some, Communion is a time to feel sad and maybe guilty or even angry at the Roman soldiers or Jewish religious leaders for what Jesus endured.

To take Communion religiously, ignorantly, and with little or no real connection to the Lord robs it of its intended purpose as well. It is taking Communion with a heart of faith in what each emblem, the bread representing the body and cup representing blood, that bears the most impact and deepens our communion with Him.

When Jesus inaugurated the Lord's Supper in connection with the New Covenant, it reflected Passover. Passover was first observed in the homes of Israelite families in Egypt the night before the exodus. Jesus celebrated the Passover meal in a home with His disciples before praying in the Garden of Gethsemane. (Matthew 26:18 KJV)

The early church also observed the Lord's Supper in homes (Acts 2:42) but not only on Passover. Jesus Himself removed the time restriction when He says *"as often as you eat this bread and drink this cup."** The words *"as often"* imply it can be as often as you would like. If knowing Him and remembering His sacrifice is something you want to do more and more, then Communion could be a wonderful way to "commune" with Him and do that.

According to Jesus, there are two significant parts of Communion or what we also call the Last Supper. Jesus' body and His blood are what we are savoring and partaking of.

> *For I pass on to you what I received from the Lord himself. On the night when he was betrayed, the Lord Jesus took some bread and gave thanks to God for it. Then he broke it in pieces and said, "This is my body, which is given for you. Do this in remembrance of me." In the same way, he took the cup of wine after supper, saying, "This cup is the new covenant between God and his people—an agreement confirmed with my blood. Do this in remembrance of me as often as you drink it"* (1 Corinthians 11:23-25 NLT).

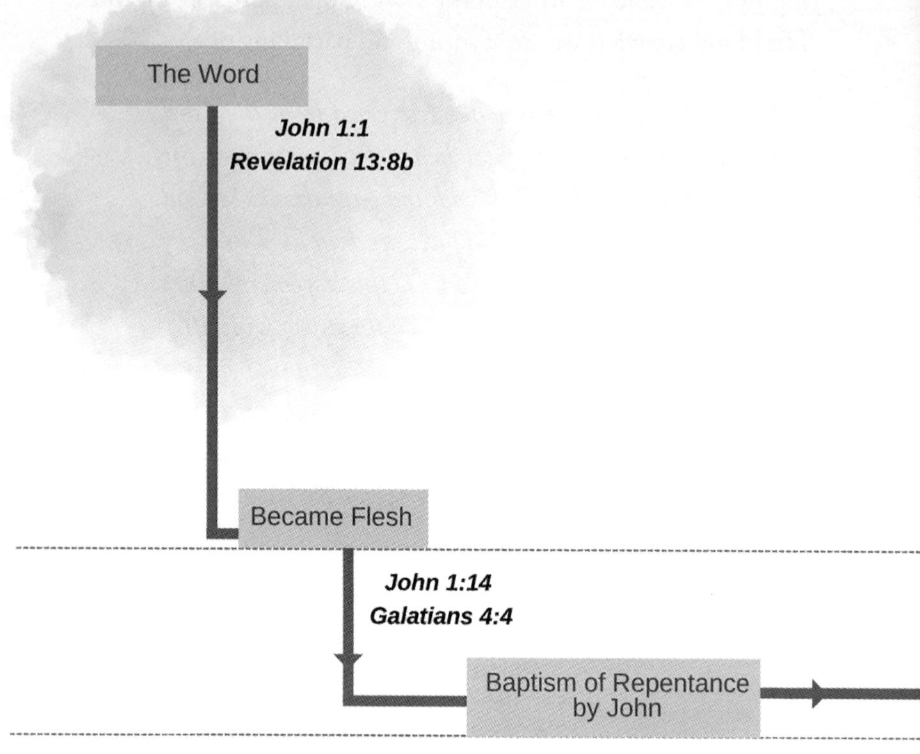
The Word
John 1:1
Revelation 13:8b
Became Flesh
John 1:14
Galatians 4:4
Baptism of Repentance by John
Matthew 3:5,6,11,13-17

Jesus' Journey to the Cross

Philippians 2:6-8 NLT

6 Though he was God, he did not think of
equality with God as something to cling to.
7 Instead, he gave up his divine privileges;
he took the humble position of a slave and was
born as a human being.
When he appeared in human form,
8 he humbled himself in obedience to God and
died a criminal's death on a cross.

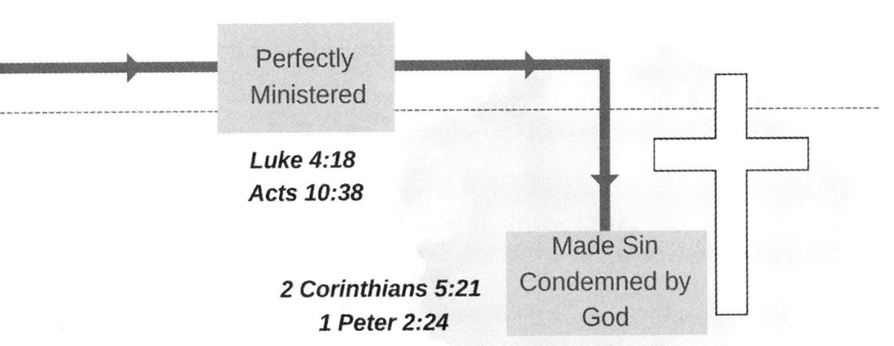

JESUS LIVED BEFORE HE DIED

Before receiving the bread and cup, there are appropriate "communion" verses that are most always used.

It was at the Passover meal celebrated by Jesus and His followers that Communion was first explained and served. The traditional Communion verses are what the Gospel writers wrote from that sacred time with Jesus, and it's not uncommon for believers to be able to quote at least a portion of them.

After Jesus served Communion, they all sang a hymn together and then went to the Garden of Gethsemane. And from that garden location there was no retreat from all that was ordained to be done to Jesus by the will of His Father.

It was when I fellowshipped with Jesus daily in Communion that He made me aware of so much more. For example, when I took Communion, instead of only considering the passion and sacrifice of Jesus' body in the last few hours of His life, I was reminded that Jesus pre-existed as the Word long before He became flesh, human. At just the right time He was born into a human body and for 33 years was exposed to temptations and the effects of sin all around Him. It was in His body that He represented His Father perfectly and ministered, powerfully anointed by the Holy Spirit throughout His final three years on earth.

Before being sacrificed, the body of every little Passover lamb up to that time had to qualify for that sacred purpose. Great care was given to protect the body of the lamb, as one blemish on it in any way would disqualify it from being a valid sacrifice. Similarly, Jesus, the Lamb of God, had to qualify to carry out the final and most important sacrifice of all. One defect, one mistake, one poor choice, one lie, one act of rebellion or disobedience would have rendered Jesus as an invalid sacrifice for our sin, because He would have become a sinner along with the rest of us.

The Father received Jesus as the perfect sacrifice for us. Not only for His perfect suffering and sacrifice but also for His perfect life that preceded His sacrifice. How worthy He is of our praise.

Part of these 31 days of devotions are dedicated to Jesus' life before His death. Remembering that the body that died first lived and with great purpose He lived.

ARE YOU READY FOR THIS?

> *For he who eats and drinks in an* ***unworthy manner*** *eats and drinks judgment to himself, not discerning the Lord's body. For this reason many are weak and sick among you, and many sleep* (1 Corinthians 11:29-30 NKJV).

Are you unworthy to take the Lord's Supper? If you have sinned, are you unworthy of taking the Lord's Supper? If you are sick, are you unworthy of taking the Lord's Supper? If you are depressed, are you unworthy of taking the Lord's Supper? No, these things actually make you a candidate to take, receive, and be changed by what Jesus suffered for. He took unto Himself these very things and suffered for you.

Notice that the scripture says "unworthy manner" not "unworthily." The *unworthy manner* of taking the Lord's Supper is one that says you don't really need what He did for you. It says that you make yourself better by your own deeds so you can take Communion. An unworthy manner is trusting anyone or anything to save, cleanse, change, and heal instead of Jesus, the Lamb of God.

Notice that it is not God who brings judgment upon a person who drinks in an unworthy manner. The person who is ignorant of that work or those who devalue or doubt it, believing it is ineffective for them, end up drinking the judgment that Jesus chose in Gethsemane to drink on their behalf. Of course, God desires that every person believe in the great work of salvation that Jesus accomplished.

> *For this is how God loved the world: He gave his one and only Son, so that everyone who believes in him will not perish but have eternal life. God sent his Son into the world not to judge the world, but to save the world through him* (John 3:16-17 NLT).

None of us are worthy of such an outpouring of the love of God that was shown in Jesus' work for us. Not by your perfection but simply by believing, receiving, and partaking can make you a recipient of Jesus' perfect sacrifice for you. If you believe, you are ready!

WHY A COMMUNION DEVOTIONAL?

This devotional is meant to be a tool to assist you in your communion with the Lord with the focus on partaking of His body and blood again and again. There are 31 opportunities for Communion in this devotional that can be used in a variety of ways.

The following are some options for use:

- Daily for one month
- Once a week
- Once a month
- Start again after finishing
- Repeat days you feel the need to focus on
- Use privately for yourself
- Use with the family, spouse, or small group
- Use in a church setting

I recommend that you prepare what you will use for the bread and cup. A piece of bread or cracker and juice are what I normally use. Each Communion devotional has a brief teaching that includes scripture. At the end of the teaching is a Communion prayer to pray that incorporates the teaching. Following Communion, I have included more verses as additional references for you to consider and meditate on, especially if you are repeating the devotional or want to glean more in a particular area. Space is given each day for your own notes as well.

So much more could be written in each entry, but I am confident that the Holy Spirit, the great Teacher, will continue to unpack more understanding of truth to you as you commune with Him again and again. Each devotional can be read and prayed in as few as five minutes or extended as long as you wish as you fellowship more with the Lord through prayer and consider the additional scriptures.

Taking a step toward knowing Him as you fellowship with Him over His body and blood will be rewarded with God coming close to you. Your fellowship with Him will be sweeter and more intimate. Expect healing and restoration where it is needed.

> *Come close to God, and God will come close to you...* (James 4:8 NLT).

The lessons in this devotional begin with the body of Jesus and then move on to focus on His blood.

Here is my prayer for you.

> *My dear heavenly Father, I pray for each person who has set their heart to know You more. You*

promised that if we seek You, we will find You if we seek You with all our hearts. Open each person's eyes to cherish through Communion the body of Jesus that You prepared and used for Your purposes. Give understanding to each heart regarding the blood every time they drink the cup. I pray that Your immense love, forgiveness, and healing will be experienced again and again and in receiving from what Jesus accomplished. And as they freely receive from You, may they freely give and extend the same goodness to others. I ask this in Jesus' precious name. Amen.

JESUS' LIFE

DAY 1

JESUS' BODY, GOD'S GIFT OF LOVE TO ME

For a child is ***born to us****, a son is* ***given to us****....*

Isaiah 9:6 NLT

There has never been a gift as significant and precious as what God gave us in the Person of Jesus. Jesus is living evidence of the great love that the Father has for us as the following verses reveal.

> *For here is the way God loved the world—he gave his only, unique Son as a gift...* (John 3:16 TPT).

> *For God has proved his love by giving us his greatest treasure, the gift of his Son...* (Romans 8:32 TPT).

Every aspect of Jesus' being is a gift of eternal value. But look how Jesus specifically drew attention to *His body* for us to remember.

> *...On the night when he was betrayed, the Lord Jesus took some bread and gave thanks to God for it. Then he broke it in pieces and said, "This is* ***my body, which is given for you.*** *Do this in remembrance of me"* (1 Corinthians 11:23-24 NLT).

Jesus' body was given to us for multiple reasons, but ultimately it was given as a sacrifice for us. Is there something about His body that we should know that would help us know and appreciate Him more?

COMMUNION

Dear Father, thank You for Your great love for me. Thank You for expressing Your love to me by giving me Your best gift. Jesus.

Show me more about the purpose of Jesus' body so I can remember and honor it appropriately, not putting it on the shelf and forgetting about it.

As I take communion now, I remember and gratefully receive the gift of Jesus' body and acknowledge His precious blood.

ADDITIONAL SCRIPTURES TO CONSIDER

Ephesians 2:4-5 NLT; 1 John 1:2; 4:16 NLT

NOTES

DAY 2

PREPARED FOR PURPOSE

Therefore, when He came into the world, He said: "Sacrifice and offering You did not desire, ***but a body You have prepared for Me."***

Hebrews 10:5 NKJV

The purpose of Jesus' first coming to earth could not be accomplished without His body. A human body. Jesus' 33 years on earth, beginning in the manger and ending in the total redemption of Adam's race, brought salvation to all the areas of mankind that were fractured by sin. This required all the physical stages of Jesus' life.

The part Jesus' body was to play in the Father's plan was not a fleeting thought in His mind but was perfectly planned before creation, before humankind existed. Hebrews 10:5 says Jesus' body was "prepared" by God. The preparation involved covenants with certain individuals and included scores of people over many generations, each playing their destined role.

Finally, in the fullness of time, the perfect time, Jesus was born of a woman. Mary, Jesus' mother, was not just some random woman but one God chose to provide the human aspect that His Word would live in. The God/Man. Incarnated.

COMMUNION

Thank You, Father, for Your great plan of redemption which required that You give Your Son to the world. I gratefully acknowledge everyone involved in Your perfect plan that led up to Jesus' birth. I pause to recognize that Jesus' conception and birth as a baby boy was strategically part of Your great plan to redeem mankind and bring us back to Yourself.

As I hold the bread today and drink the cup, I acknowledge Jesus' entire and perfectly planned life that each represents and thank You for planning it all.

ADDITIONAL SCRIPTURES TO CONSIDER

Genesis 3:15; Isaiah 7:14; Luke 1-3 NLT; John 1:14; Philippians 2:7-8 NLT; Hebrews 2:14; Galatians 4:4-5; Romans 1:2-4 NLT; 9:4-5 NLT; 1 Timothy 3:16; 1 John 1:1-3 NLT

NOTES

DAY 3

EXPOSED

So the Word became human and made his home among us....

John 1:14 NLT

Jesus wasn't born in a time of history when the nation of Israel was at its spiritual peak or in its most prosperous state. The fullness of time for Him to be born was when Israel was struggling under Roman occupation. Jesus also didn't live above us in a place of privilege that insulated and shielded Him from human sufferings. No, before He was anointed by the Holy Spirit to bring healing and deliverance, He physically lived among us for 30 years, intentionally exposing His senses to the effects of human sin, difficulties, and the pain that sin caused.

Jesus experienced how political injustice affected people He loved. He saw sick and crippled people and the cruel effects of poverty. He grew up hearing people cry because of their suffering. Words of anger and abuse were not foreign to His ears. He smelled disease that wasted the flesh and the terrible consequences of sin and of demonic oppression.

By the time Jesus went to the Cross, He was well aware of and thoroughly acquainted with what it was that He was going to have to bear.

COMMUNION

My dear heavenly Father, thank You for Your amazing plan of redemption. Jesus, thank You for not resisting the life that God's plan required You to experience. You didn't withdraw and hide Your eyes from the conditions of fallen humanity. As I hold this bread in my hand and as I drink this cup today, I am so grateful that You lived as a person among us and were thoroughly exposed to everything that eventually You would save us from.

ADDITIONAL SCRIPTURES TO CONSIDER

Galatians 4:4-5 NLT; Isaiah 50:4 AMPC

NOTES

DAY 4

EXPOSED BUT NOT CONTAMINATED

The Bible says this: "He never did anything that was wrong. He never said anything that was not true."

1 Peter 2:22 EASY

This High Priest of ours understands our weaknesses, for he faced all of the same testings we do, yet he did not sin.

Hebrews 4:15 NLT

Sacrificing babies has been a practice of many pagan religions to please or appease their gods. If being sacrificed for our sins was the single detail that the mission of Jesus' first coming to earth entailed, it could have easily taken place when he was a baby.

But a baby could not have faced all the temptations that humans do. Jesus was required to face what a child, a teenager, a young man, and a fully mature man faces. To identify with humans, He was tempted with every kind of temptation to sin but never yielded to sin.

Galatians 5:19-21 (NLT) lists sins of the flesh as *"sexual immorality, impurity, lustful pleasures, idolatry, sorcery, hostility, quarreling, jealousy, outbursts of anger, selfish ambition, dissension, division, envy, drunkenness, wild parties, and other sins like these."* Temptations to these and all other kinds of sin were what Jesus was intentionally exposed to.

The temptations were intensified in the wilderness when Satan *himself* tempted Jesus.

Instead of ever doing what seemed pleasing to Himself in the moment, Jesus lived every one of His moments to only please His Father.

COMMUNION

Precious Jesus. As I hold this bread representing Your body, I thank You for never giving in to the temptation to sin. Not even once. Thank You for living perfectly in Your body. Thank You for Your perfect blood as well. Today I praise You for staying pure.

ADDITIONAL SCRIPTURES TO CONSIDER

Luke 2:51-52 NLT; 4:1-13 NLT;
John 12:49 NLT; Hebrews 2:17-18 NLT

NOTES

DAY 5

JESUS IDENTIFIED WITH HUMANS

Because God's children are human beings—made of flesh and blood—the Son also became ***flesh and blood....***

Hebrews 2:14 NLT

Redeeming mankind required that Jesus identify with us. He not only came to us, He totally identified with us. The first step in that identification was Jesus becoming flesh and blood, human.

The next step was that Jesus had to identify with fallen humanity without falling Himself. We see that He did this successfully in His perfect life as well as what took place in His baptism by John, which was known as a baptism of repentance. Let's be clear. Jesus had nothing to repent of. He had no sin, yet He insisted that He had to participate in this baptism for identification with people who were repenting of their sins.

> *And when they confessed their sins, he* [John] *baptized them in the Jordan River. ...Then Jesus went from Galilee to the Jordan River to be baptized by John. But John tried to talk him out of it. "I am the one who needs to be baptized by you," he said, "so why are you coming to me?" But Jesus said, "It should be done, for we must carry out all that God requires..."* (Matthew 3:6,13-15 NLT).

It was after Jesus explained that God required this baptism of repentance of Him that John agreed to baptize Jesus.

Why in the world did God require that Jesus be baptized in a baptism of repentance from sin when He had never once yielded to sin? Was this another step of obedience to identify with fallen sinful humanity? I believe so.

> *After his baptism* [of repentance from sin], *as Jesus came up out of the water, the heavens were opened and he saw the Spirit of God descending like a dove and settling on him. And a voice from heaven said, "This is my dearly loved Son, who brings me great joy"* (Matthew 3:16-17 NLT).

So Jesus was immersed (baptized) into His identification with fallen humanity, all in obedience to God. Everyone else was being baptized because of their repented disobedience. By contrast, it was because of Jesus' willing obedience to God that He was baptized in this particular baptism of repentance, which brought His Father great joy.

COMMUNION

Dear Lord Jesus, as I hold the bread today that represents Your body, I praise You for carrying out the Father's plan of redemption in every detail. Thank You for becoming one with me, a human, in my fallen and broken state, as this baptism pictured. Thank You for identifying with sinners without sinning and without contaminating Your precious blood through disobedience to the Father. I thank You today for the obedient participation of Your body and for Your blood to all of our Father's will.

ADDITIONAL SCRIPTURES TO CONSIDER

Luke 3:3 NLT; Acts 19:3-5 NLT;
Hebrews 2:17-18 NLT; Philippians 2:6-11 NLT

NOTES

JESUS' REPRESENTATION OF THE FATHER

DAY 6

FLAWLESS REPRESENTATION

In the past God spoke to our ancestors through the prophets at many times and in various ways, but in these last days he has spoken to us by his Son, whom he appointed heir of all things, and through whom also he made the universe. The Son is the radiance of God's glory and the exact representation of his being....

Hebrews 1:1-3 NIV

What was God like? Was He like Moses? Noah? Joshua? Samuel? David? All of these and other people of the Old Testament were set apart for specific purposes to represent and demonstrate God to others. While the Holy Spirit came on them to enable them to accomplish His purposes, God did not live in any of them. They were able to represent God in a limited and assigned area, but they sadly misrepresented Him in other ways.

By these misrepresentations and the lack of revelation about God Himself, there would have been all kinds of wrong conclusions and opinions of what God was like. Jesus rectified and clarified it all by perfectly representing and demonstrating His Father's will and nature throughout His entire life.

We can look at these and others who were used of God in the Old Testament and contrast them with Jesus and see something very interesting. Being used of God and actually being God are obviously and distinctly two different things.

> *We proclaim to you the one who existed from the beginning, whom we have heard and seen. We saw him with our own eyes and touched him with our own hands. He is the Word of life. This one who is life itself was revealed to us, and we have seen him. And now we testify and proclaim to you that he is the one who is eternal life. He was with the Father, and then he was revealed to us. We proclaim to you what we ourselves have actually seen and heard so that you may have fellowship with us. And our fellowship is with the Father and with his Son, Jesus Christ* (1 John 1:1-3 NLT).

> *"If you had known Me, you would have known My Father also...." Jesus said to him, ..."He who has seen Me has seen the Father..."* (John 14:7,9 NKJV).

COMMUNION

Dear heavenly Father, I worship You for providing a perfect representation for Yourself on earth. In my Communion today, I acknowledge that by all Jesus said and did in His body during His time on earth, I can not only come to know Jesus but also know who You, my Father, truly are. Jesus, I worship You for perfectly representing the Father every day of Your life. I thank You today for Your body, and I thank You for Your blood.

ADDITIONAL SCRIPTURES TO CONSIDER

John 1:14 NLT; 5:30 NLT; Hebrews 2:14 NLT

NOTES

DAY 7

PERFECT MINISTRY

And you know that God anointed Jesus of Nazareth with the Holy Spirit and with power. Then Jesus went around doing good and healing all who were oppressed by the devil, for God was with him.

Acts 10:38 NLT

After 30 years of intentional and perfect living among humanity, Jesus began to minister.

The Gospels record the three years of Jesus' supernatural ministry after He was anointed of the Holy Spirit. All of this divine ministry happened through God's unhindered use of Jesus' body. What Jesus' eyes saw and His ears heard moved Him with divine compassion, resulting in teaching, food multiplication, and healing of all kinds of maladies.

Healing virtue came through Jesus' hands when He laid them on the sick. The sick connected with that same virtue whenever they touched Jesus' body in faith.

His voice, his mouth, communicated His Father's words and His dominion over demons and nature. While He never yielded His body to sin, he continuously yielded His body for His Father's will to be demonstrated in ministry.

Jesus' teachings utilized real-life examples that everyone could understand. He was able to take kingdom realities and make them applicable to the daily life of a human.

COMMUNION

Dear Lord Jesus, today as I commune with You over the bread and cup, I acknowledge the Father's will in Your ministry could only be achieved through Your body. I take time to imagine Your eyes, ears, Your hands, and Your feet were all used to express the Father's love, healing and delivering power. I worship You for continually offering Your body for this purpose. I eat and partake now of the bread and drink the cup that represents Your yielded body and blood.

ADDITIONAL SCRIPTURES TO CONSIDER

Matthew 8:16 NLT; Luke 4:18 NLT;
Philippians 2:7 NLT

NOTES

JESUS' BODY

DAY 8

THE PINNACLE OF JESUS' ASSIGNMENT—FULFILLING THE WILL OF GOD

The old system under the law of Moses was only a shadow, a dim preview of the good things to come, not the good things themselves. The sacrifices under that system were repeated again and again, year after year, but they were never able to provide perfect cleansing for those who came to worship. If they could have provided perfect cleansing, the sacrifices would have stopped, for the worshipers would have been purified once for all time, and their feelings of guilt would have disappeared. But instead, those sacrifices actually reminded them of their sins year after year. For it is not possible for the blood of bulls and goats to take away sins. That is why, when Christ came into the world, he said to God, "You did not want animal sacrifices or sin offerings. ***But you have given me a body to offer."***

Hebrews 10:1-5 NLT

Jesus' body was prepared by God to live among people, and He became famous through His ministry to them. While fulfilling the law each day of His life was also essential to Jesus' mission, representing Moses and the Law was never His ultimate goal. Jesus fulfilled the Law by daily representing and pleasing the Father, and that fulfillment qualified Jesus for His paramount task of obedience to the Father.

In the same way animal sacrifices in the Old Covenant had to be perfect to qualify to be offered, Jesus, the Lamb of God, was truly perfect in every way, qualifying Him for His final act of obedience, which was to be sacrificed on behalf of sinful humanity.

Lambs were one of the animals used in Old Covenant sacrifices. There were also bulls, goats, sheep, and birds whose bodies without defect, representing innocent lives, were taken on behalf of the guilty. Their purpose becomes a way we can understand the purpose of Jesus' body and His blood.

The sacrifice of animals happened daily but could never accomplish what the one-time sacrifice that the Lamb of God did. Our redemption.

COMMUNION

Precious Lamb of God, thank You for not stopping short of Your ultimate mission to save me through the sacrifice of Your body and shedding of Your blood. As I take Communion now, I remember gratefully that You fulfilled everything necessary during Your life to qualify to die for me.

ADDITIONAL SCRIPTURES TO CONSIDER

Isaiah 53:7,10; Acts 8:32; Philippians 2:7-8; John 1:29; 1 Peter 1:18-20; 1 Corinthians 5:7; Revelation 5:12

NOTES

DAY 9

HE TOOK MY PLACE

Lay your hand on the animal's head, and the Lord will accept its death in your place to purify you, making you right with him.

Leviticus 1:4 NLT

Leviticus chapters 1 to 9 detail various sacrifices and their purpose. The instruction in the scripture above is repeated for every type of sacrifice.

Why was the person offering an animal to be sacrificed instructed to lay his hand on the head of the animal before its life was taken? One reason is that by laying their hand on the animal's head, the person is saying, "I sinned and deserve sin's punishment—death. This animal is dying in my place because I sinned. I claim this animal's death on my behalf."

With every sacrifice, the reality that an innocent animal was the substitute for the individual(s) who sinned told the story of the ultimate coming sacrifice. Jesus. Perfect in every way, He would die for all who are guilty of sin.

COMMUNION

My Jesus, as I hold this piece of bread in my hand today, I acknowledge that the punishment of my sin was death and that You died in my place. I didn't die for my own sin but I am so grateful that You were punished for my sin and actually died in my place. I acknowledge with this cup that You bled for me. Through taking my punishment and shedding Your blood for me, You purchased me. My life now belongs to You.

ADDITIONAL SCRIPTURES TO CONSIDER

Leviticus 3:2,8,13; 4:4,15,24,29,33;
8:14,18,22; 16:21;
Isaiah 53:4-6; Romans 6:23; 1 Corinthians 6:19-20;
2 Corinthians 5:21; 1 Peter 2:24

NOTES

DAY 10

THE BODY OF THE SACRIFICE

He will lay both of his hands on the goat's head and confess over it all the wickedness, rebellion, and sins of the people of Israel. In this way, he will transfer the people's sins to the head of the goat....

Leviticus 16:21 NLT

This instruction is part of all that was to happen on the Day of Atonement. While the high priest lays his hands on the head of the goat, he also confesses over it all the wickedness, rebellion, and sins of the people.

The added instruction in today's verse of confessing sins helps us know what happened when a person laid a hand on the head of the sacrifice. With this action, the sins of the individual(s) were transferred to the animal and the innocent body of the animal to be sacrificed served as a rubbish bin or dumping ground. God designated the body of the animal to be sacrificed as the location for the sin to be dumped. After sin was transferred to the animal, that sin was judged when the life of the animal was taken.

In the same way, with each blow, every possible thing wrong with fallen mankind was laid on Jesus in entirety by the Father.

> *...the Lord laid on him the sins of us all* (Isaiah 53:6 NLT).

> *...And God has piled all our sins, everything we've done wrong, on him, on him* (Isaiah 53:6 MSG).

The next verse pictures Jesus' body as the container for our sins as well:

> *For God took the sinless Christ and poured into Him our sins...* (2 Corinthians 5:21 TLB).

COMMUNION

Dear Father God, today as I eat the bread and drink the cup, I acknowledge that not only did You use Jesus' body for Your healing and delivering power to flow through, but that same perfect body was where You piled our sins. You put all of our sins on Jesus; and as a result, He became sin. Oh what an act of love! Jesus, thank You, for bearing it all for me and for all of humanity. As I eat the bread and drink the cup, I picture and believe that all that is wrong about me was put on Jesus.

ADDITIONAL SCRIPTURES TO CONSIDER

Isaiah 53:10-11; 2 Corinthians 5:21 NIV;
1 Peter 2:24 NIV

NOTES

DAY 11

SIN IS PUNISHED

The Law that God gave to Moses could not make us free like that. We were too weak to obey his Law because we are human. But God has done what his Law could not do. He sent his own Son to become a person like us. His human body was like the body of people who do wrong things. God's Son died as a sacrifice to take away the punishment for our sins. In that way, God destroyed the power of sin over people who are weak and human.

Romans 8:3 EASY

The ordeal of sacrifice for the animal was as humane as possible. When sin was transferred to the head of the animal, it was with words. There was no torture, abuse, or pain inflicted on the animal. When the life of the animal was taken by a brief slit to the throat, it yielded its blood to cover sin. Hebrews 10:11 says that the animal's blood could not take sin away, however.

The torture that was not required of any sacrifice animal's body was required of Jesus' body. Sin was not only put on Jesus, but Jesus also experienced the awful punishment for that sin.

> *But it was our sins that did that to him, that ripped and tore and crushed him—our sins! He took the punishment, and that made us whole* (Isaiah 53:5 MSG).

In Jesus' body, God dealt with the sin, all that was wrong with us. With zero tolerance for sin, He did NOT say "whatever you feel is right is okay with me. You're fine the way you are. Everyone sins. I'll look the other way." No. Absolutely not! Instead, He took sin from us and put it on Jesus, and it was on the body of His Son that God judged and punished our sin.

Our sin was not excused or in any way tolerated—it was thoroughly condemned when God's judgment was expressed by what happened to Jesus' body. How does God feel about sin? Look at Jesus' torn and mutilated body on the Cross. God is not okay with sin that destroys any area of our life and separates us from Him. Jesus took the punishment and judgment for our sin. Praise Him forever.

COMMUNION

Dear God, as I hold the bread and cup today, I am aware that they symbolize not only the body and the blood, but also the punishment for my sin and price of forgiveness. In order to have mercy on me, You had to judge my sin on Your Son. To honor this great act, I believe and gratefully receive the love that motivated it. Praise the Lord, oh my soul, who forgives all my sin and heals all my disease.

ADDITIONAL SCRIPTURES TO CONSIDER

Psalm 103:2-3; Hebrews 10:10;
Isaiah 52:13; 53:5; 2 Corinthians 5:21;
1 Peter 3:18

NOTES

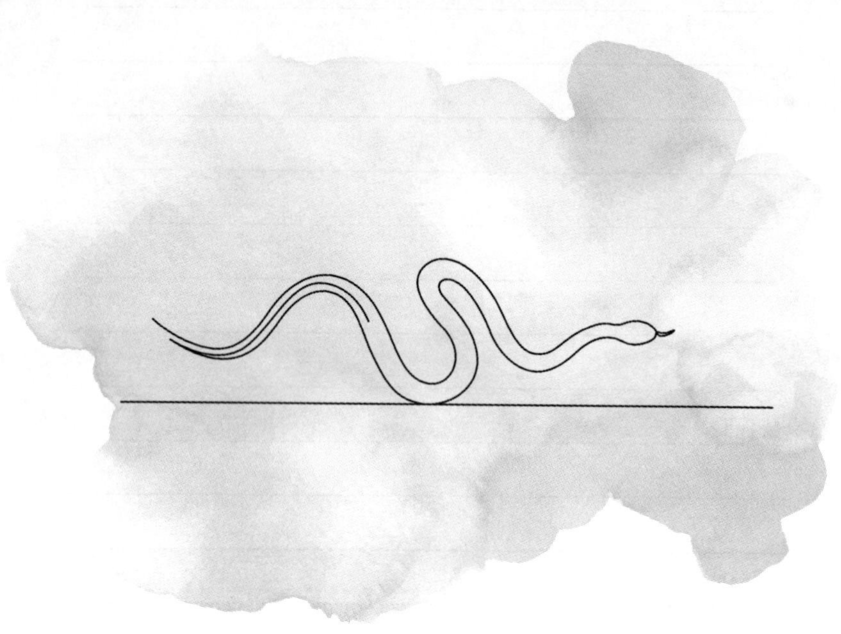

DAY 12

THE SERPENT ON THE POLE

And as Moses lifted up the serpent in the wilderness, even so must the Son of Man be lifted up.

John 3:14 NKJV

Calling Jesus the serpent on the pole was not a cruel accusation from a mean person. No, Jesus identified Himself as the serpent on the pole. But how can that be? Jesus was perfect and a serpent generally represents sin, sin's curse and all things evil.

The following verses explain this strange picture of Jesus.

> *For He* [God] *made Him* [Jesus] *who knew no sin to be sin for us...* (2 Corinthians 5:21 NKJV).

Jesus didn't become sin by something bad *He* did. He became sin when God put on Him *our* sin.

In addition to sin, the serpent also represents the consequences of sin that the Bible calls "the curse."

> *Christ has redeemed us from the curse of the law, having* ***become a curse*** *for us (for it is written, "Cursed is everyone who hangs on a tree")* (Galatians 3:13 NKJV).

It was when Jesus' body was hung on the Cross that He became the curse.

What is the curse anyway?

The curse was consequences that came as a result of breaking God's laws. The list in Deuteronomy 28 of these horrible curses that could be expected include all kinds of sicknesses and diseases in the body, mental illnesses, family tragedy, and financial disaster.

In the same way that roaches, mice, rats, and other vermin are drawn to rubbish and filth, the curse comes to sin. You can certainly see why the serpent is definitely a good representation of the curse that Jesus became.

The pole represented the Cross, and the serpent pictured Jesus when He became sin and sin's curse. Because brass in the Bible symbolizes judgment, the brass pole and serpent also represents the judgment of God that fell on our sin and the curse as Jesus hung on the Cross.

COMMUNION

My blessed Lord Jesus, after living spotlessly, You became sin as well as the curse that comes as a result of sin. Thank You for saying yes and receiving this when the Father put it on You so that I can say no to sin and sin's curse now. As I take Communion today, I honor You for becoming sin and the curse and for receiving judgment from God on the Cross that should have been mine. I boldly say "NO" to sin and sin's curse. Jesus bore it for me so I absolutely refuse to bear it again.

ADDITIONAL SCRIPTURES TO CONSIDER

Numbers 21:4-9 NLT; Galatians 3:13 NLT

NOTES

DAY 13

GAZING AT THE SERPENT

And the Lord said to Moses, Make a fiery serpent [of bronze] and set it on a pole; and everyone who is bitten, when he looks at it, shall live.

Numbers 21:8 AMPC

In this true story, a natural reaction to poisonous snakes slithering on the ground could have been to run. But run where?! Snakes were everywhere. Or how about grabbing something to beat the snakes to death? There were too many. It would have certainly been tempting to be distracted by the poisonous serpents and their bites. But the promise for life depended on each persons' steady, expectant, absorbing gaze. And what were they to look at? It was not the snakes slithering around them but the immovable brass serpent on the pole. The best way for them to help their loved ones who had been bitten was to help them look at that same serpent on the pole.

You may be tempted to gaze at the "snakes" in your life. Perhaps there are alarming symptoms in your body or other threats to you and your loved ones' well-being. Whatever holds your attention is what is affecting you. What are you looking at?

> *And Moses made a serpent of bronze and put it on a pole, and if a serpent had bitten any man, when he looked to the serpent of bronze [attentively, expectantly, with a steady and absorbing gaze], he lived* (Numbers 21:9 AMPC).

Make sure you are looking attentively, expectantly, with a steady and absorbing gaze at the right snake. That would be the One lifted up on the pole (Cross) so that whoever believes in the work that He did on the Cross would not perish, but live! What things in your life do you need to look away from? What aspects of Jesus do you need to gaze upon today?

COMMUNION

As I take Communion today, my Savior, help me look away from what's wrong with my body to Yours as You hung on that Cross. Help me see that anything wrong with me was poured into You and was judged there. Help me to gaze, not just glance, at this amazing work of divine love until it becomes more real to me than the "snakes." I eat the bread and drink the cup declaring that Jesus took and became a curse for me.

ADDITIONAL SCRIPTURES TO CONSIDER

James 1:25 NLT; 1 Peter 1:12 NLT; 2:24 NLT;
2 Corinthians 3:18; 5:21 NLT

NOTES

DAY 14

I SANCTIFY MYSELF

And so for their sake and on their behalf
I sanctify (dedicate, consecrate) Myself,
that they also may be sanctified (dedicated,
consecrated, made holy) in the Truth.

John 17:19 AMPC

Jesus' sanctified life of dedication and obedience to God qualified Him to sanctify us. What does that mean? To sanctify means to separate, divide from the rest, to consecrate to holy purpose.

Jesus' sanctified life and death, completely dedicated to God's purpose for Him, made a way for us to be sanctified and dedicated to God's purpose for our own lives as well.

Hebrews 10:10 (NLT) says *"For God's will was for us to be made holy by the sacrifice of the body of Jesus Christ, once for all time."*

This one-time offering of Jesus' body was sufficient to sanctify every human from the defects of sin on our spirit, soul, and body. That sacrifice has the ability to separate us from every dysfunction, weakness, sickness, disease, and anything less than God's original intention for us. It also has the ability to separate us to God's purpose for our lives as it says in the following verse:

> *He sacrificed himself for us that he might purchase our freedom from every lawless deed and to purify for himself a people who are his very own, passionate to do what is beautiful in his eyes* (Titus 2:14 TPT).

COMMUNION

Dear Jesus, my Sanctifier, by Your sacrifice not only did You separate me from everything wicked but You also separated me to the Father's purpose for my life. You have purified me to do Your will with all my heart. As I take Communion today, I acknowledge that because Jesus lived a life dedicated to God—spirit, soul, and body—He has separated me to do the same. I choose God's will for my life.

ADDITIONAL SCRIPTURES TO CONSIDER

1 Corinthians 1:30; Exodus 29:33 AMPC

NOTES

DAY 15

THE BODY CARRIED THE BLOOD

Wherefore Jesus also, that he might sanctify the people with his own blood, suffered without the gate.

Hebrews 13:12 KJV

Although Jesus' physical genes would have been a combination of Mary's and the Holy Spirit's (with God, nothing is impossible), His blood didn't come from either. The marrow in the bones of a fetus actually makes the blood that its little heart begins to pump. Jesus' blood came from the marrow in His own bones, forever connecting Jesus' body to His blood. The body and the blood worked together to sanctify us from the kingdom of darkness to the kingdom of light.

Although Jesus' body was thoroughly ripped open, exposing His bones, not one of them was broken. His bones, the part of His body having to do with the production of redemption's price— the blood—were kept protected.

Not only did Jesus' body house the ransom blood like a vault keeps valuable treasure, but Jesus also kept the blood that ran through His veins pure and uncontaminated by never committing sin. All the years of Jesus' earthly life, from the time His fetal heart began to pump blood till His blood gushed out of His body starting in the Garden of Gethsemane and ending on Golgotha's hill, He kept Himself from the contamination of sin for us. Jesus' blood could only qualify to pay our ransom if, unlike ours, it was holy, uncontaminated from sin. And it was.

COMMUNION

Today as I hold the bread and cup, I worship the Great Planner of redemption. Your Son's blood is the price for our total redemption, and I praise Him for keeping His blood pure through living obediently to You. I am redeemed, and I say so! I'm redeemed from darkness and to Your glorious light and divine purpose for my life. I am redeemed by the blood of Jesus!

ADDITIONAL SCRIPTURES TO CONSIDER

Psalm 107:2; 34:20;
1 Peter 1:18-19 EASY; Hebrews 13:12 GNT

NOTES

JESUS' SUFFERING

DAY 16

HE TOOK THE CUP

And he took a cup of wine and gave thanks to God for it. He gave it to them and said, "Each of you drink from it, for this is my blood, which confirms the covenant between God and his people. It is poured out as a sacrifice to forgive the sins of many."

Matthew 26:27-28 NLT

Unlike the Old Mosaic Covenant that was etched in stone, the conditions and benefits of the New Covenant were carved in the body of the Redeemer and required a signature. The required signature to ratify the covenant was the blood of Jesus, testifying of everything that was accomplished in the sacrifice of His body.

Safely carrying the blood, redemption's price, was in itself a massive accomplishment. However, that price had to be paid, which meant that the blood had to be poured out of His body. We'll look at how that happened as we continue.

COMMUNION

Dear Lord Jesus, the New Covenant was not signed with my blood, my perfection, or my sacrifice. It was confirmed with Your perfect blood that came from Your perfect body. Every detail of this covenant was carved in Your body, and Your blood signed it. It is finished and done. Lord, as I take Communion today, I pray that You open my eyes to see what belongs to me as a result of this covenant that I'm a recipient of.

ADDITIONAL SCRIPTURES TO CONSIDER

1 Corinthians 11:25; Hebrews 12:24; 9:18

NOTES

DAY 17

BLOOD IN THE GARDEN

And being in an agony [of mind], He prayed [all the] more earnestly and intently, and His sweat became like great clots of blood dropping down upon the ground.

Luke 22:44 AMPC

Defying God and willfully choosing against His instruction started in Eden's Garden. That sin was the beginning of spiritual death and all the repercussions of it.

The first place where redemptive blood flowed indicated Jesus' own struggle with the will of God in the Garden of Gethsemane. Bear in mind, Jesus experienced this spiritual and mental torture before He was ever struck physically, resulting in bloody sweat.

The spiritual horror of becoming sin, becoming sin's curse and of His Father's wrath being poured on Him, is what Jesus faced when He pled for the cup to pass from Him. These are some of the words from the Gospel writers to describe Jesus' struggle: terror, amazement, deeply troubled, depressed, exceedingly sad, overwhelmed with grief so that it almost kills me, and distress of mind. These words would never have described Jesus before His struggle in Gethsemane.

Unlike the first Adam who chose to defy God's will, Jesus, the last Adam, chose differently. Redemption's work was leveraged through Jesus' surrendered will, His choice, as He made this defining statement three times: *"Nevertheless, not My will, but Yours, be done"* (Luke 22:42 NKJV). Everything that would occur spiritually and physically to Jesus, including His torture, crucifixion, death, and burial, was fully realized and agreed to in those words.

The blood that came from Jesus' body in the garden testified that redemption would go all the way back to the fall of man. It testifies now that the first Adam's willful choice against God doesn't have to be mine. Now, like the Last Adam, Jesus, I can relinquish my own way and choose to believe, to follow, and to obey the will of God today.

COMMUNION

Father God, today as I take Communion, I choose Your will for my life. There is no other purpose more important to me than Yours. I choose to obey Your word over any other influence or opportunity. Adam and Eve chose against Your will; but

Jesus, I worship You for choosing Your Father's will to drink the cup that meant being sacrificed and bleeding for me. Your blood in the garden testifies of Your choice for Your Father's will. Thank You, Lord Jesus.

ADDITIONAL SCRIPTURES TO CONSIDER

Matthew 26:27-28 AMP; Mark 13:33 AMP

NOTES AND QUESTION FOR REFLECTION

How did Jesus' willingness to choose the Father's will for His life pave the way for you to choose God's will for your life?

DAY 18

BEATEN, BATTERED, AND BRUISED

Now the men who held Jesus mocked Him and beat Him. And having blindfolded Him, they ***struck*** *Him on the face and asked Him, saying, "Prophesy! Who is the one who struck You?"*

Luke 22:63-64 NKJV

The word *struck* (Greek, *daero*) in this verse means to be beaten until the skin is broken.

> *...He was bruised for our iniquities...* (Isaiah 53:5 NKJV).

Our iniquities were the cause for all the ways that Jesus' body was abused, beaten, and bruised before He was crucified.

Iniquities in Hebrew is the word *avon,* which is described as evil, perversity, moral distortion, and perversion of God's law, plus its consequences and punishment. This includes sexual distortion and perversion that a person has done or has been the victim of. A corresponding Greek word (G458) *anemia,* adds lawlessness to that list.

Just as iniquity shames and damages a person both inside and outside, Jesus' blood flowed internally and externally to redeem and restore. What areas of your life, both internal (unseen) and external (seen) need the application of the blood of Jesus today?

COMMUNION

Jesus, as I hold the bread and the cup, I gratefully remember that it was the cruel beating on Your body that caused redemptive blood to flow both externally and internally. Your precious blood testifies that your skin was broken and You were bruised as a result of being beaten and punished for my iniquities and the shame they caused. I worship and praise You for this.

ADDITIONAL SCRIPTURES TO CONSIDER

Mark 14:65; Isaiah 50:5-6 NLT; 52:13-14

NOTES

DAY 19

THE CRUEL CROWN

They stripped him and put a scarlet robe on him. ***They wove thorn branches into a crown and put it on his head,*** *and they placed a reed stick in his right hand as a scepter. Then they knelt before him in mockery and taunted, "Hail! King of the Jews!" And they spit on him and grabbed the stick and struck him on the head with it.*

Matthew 27:28-30 NLT

This fake coronation, meant to mock Jesus, included a crown. A crown of thorns. When this crown was pushed onto Jesus' head, the thorns pierced into Him excruciatingly.

Depression, oppression, anxiety and panic, brain dysfunctions, including all forms of mental illness that torment, are horrific to bear. Among the curses of Deuteronomy 28, these mental torments make a person wish it was day when it is night and wish it were night when it is day. It often makes the suffering person wish for death.

The crown Jesus wore symbolizes this cruel torment. The blood flowed from His blessed head as He experienced the crown's agony.

COMMUNION

Lord Jesus, I hold and take the bread and cup today again with deep gratitude. In accepting the cruel crown of thorns You wore, You also accepted all mental dysfunction, damage, illness, and conditions, all bringing torment. I acknowledge the blood from Jesus' head that testifies that I am free. I declare that same testimony. I AM FREE!

ADDITIONAL SCRIPTURES TO CONSIDER

1 Peter 2:25; Deuteronomy 28:20, 28-29, 34, 65-67; Isaiah 53:5

NOTES

DAY 20

THE STRIPES

Then Pilate had Jesus ***flogged*** *with a lead-tipped whip.*

John 19:1 NLT

...He was ***whipped*** *so we could be healed.*

Isaiah 53:5 NLT

...We are healed by the ***punishment*** *he suffered, made whole by the* ***blows*** *he received.*

Isaiah 53:5 GNT

...By his wounds [**stripes**] *you are healed.*

1 Peter 2:24 NLT

Tradition describes the Roman flogging as a gruesome and mutilating torture, and it was here that Jesus took on our sickness and infirmity and carried our diseases. In the same way He didn't resist scourging from a Roman soldier, He also didn't resist the sickness and disease that was simultaneously being laid on Him by His Father so that we could be completely healed.

COMMUNION

Jesus, as I hold the bread and the cup today, I remember how the Father put on You my sickness and disease. Putting this on You was His will that You agreed to. So now I have the right to say "no" to sickness and disease. The blood that flowed from all those stripes testifies that I AM HEALED!

ADDITIONAL SCRIPTURES TO CONSIDER

Psalm 129:3; Matthew 8:17 AMP

NOTES

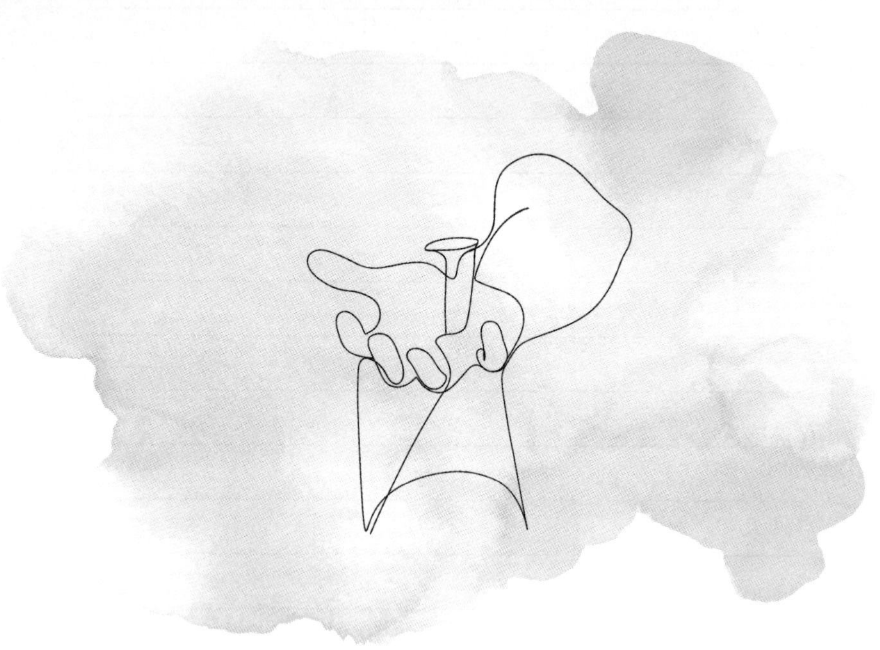

DAY 21

THE NAILS

But he was ***pierced*** *for our transgressions....*

Isaiah 53:5 NIV

T*ransgression* carries the heavy meaning of rebelling and conveys the idea of a willful and deliberate act of defiance against authority. It was for transgression that all of us have done in some way that Jesus was pierced.

> *When they came to a place called The Skull, they* ***nailed*** *him to the cross. And the criminals were also crucified—one on his right and one on his left* (Luke 23:33 NLT).

The hands that had given healing and life to people were pierced, nailed to the Cross. The beautiful feet that only days earlier had been anointed and bowed before had also taken Jesus to every place, every city, and every village His Father sent Him. This day, these feet walked obediently to awful Golgotha, where a nail securely fastened them to the Cross.

COMMUNION

Precious Lord and Savior. As I hold the bread and cup today, I remember how Your hands and feet were pierced for any rebellion and defiance against God I have had. Your blood flowed freely as a result and testified that Jesus took my punishment and place on the Cross. As a result, I am forgiven, justified, made righteous. I am forever grateful.

ADDITIONAL SCRIPTURES TO CONSIDER

Isaiah 53:12 NLT; John 20:24-29

NOTES

DAY 22

IT IS FINISHED

When Jesus had tasted it, he said, "It is finished!" Then he bowed his head and gave up his spirit.

John 19:30 NLT

What was finished? 1. Every single detail of the mission that the Father sent Jesus to earth to do was accomplished. 2. The sacrifice for the forgiveness of sin was totally accomplished for all time. No more sacrifices are required. 3. The reservoir of redemptive blood flowed until it could flow no more. 4. The curse was completely neutralized when Jesus embodied it. 5. Everything presented in the Old Covenant was fulfilled, and the New Covenant in His blood was introduced. 6. All that Jesus could do in response and obedience to the Father through His body in life, words, ministry, and finally in sacrifice, was finished. All that remained was to die. 7. Every prophecy about Jesus was fulfilled.

There were no defensive wounds on His body. He didn't try to protect Himself but freely gave His body and blood to God's will to the entirety of His life.

COMMUNION

Dearest Jesus, You did it all. This bread represents the total use of Your body in my place and as my sacrifice. This blood speaks that truly it is finished. Nothing more could be added to how You gave yourself for my salvation. I praise You today with all my heart!

ADDITIONAL SCRIPTURES TO CONSIDER

Hebrews 9:12; Colossians 1:4; Isaiah 50:6-7

NOTES

DAY 23

THE RIVEN SIDE

...one of the soldiers pierced Jesus' side with a spear, bringing a sudden flow of blood and water. The man who saw it has given testimony, and his testimony is true. He knows that he tells the truth, and he testifies so that you also may believe.

John 19:34-35 NIV

After saying, "It is finished," Jesus breathed His last breath, His perfect heart beating until there was no more blood left. In an effort to make certain Jesus was dead, a soldier pierced His side. The water and blood that flowed out was a certain physical evidence that He had already died. John gave testimony that, in fact, happened.

The last trace of Jesus' priceless blood came out through his riven side. *Riven* means to split or tear apart violently. Not only does the Bible document that Jesus' side was riven, but also that the curtain in the temple dividing the Holy Place from the Most Holy Place was torn or riven from top to bottom. We are invited to go through this open curtain as we draw near to God.

> *...a new and living way opened for us through the curtain, that is, his body, and since we have a great priest over the house of God, let us draw near to God with a sincere heart and with the full assurance that faith brings, having our hearts sprinkled to cleanse us from a guilty conscience and having our bodies washed with pure water* (Hebrews 10:20-22 NIV).

The final blood that came out of Jesus' torn side introduced another fountain flowing from Jesus that we could experience once He was glorified. That fountain, Jesus says, is the Holy Spirit and that we could come to Him and drink freely. The blood and the Holy Spirit both function and forever flow together in their testimony of Jesus' immaculate work.

COMMUNION

Dear Jesus, today as I take the bread and cup, I acknowledge that You gave everything for me. Your blood testifies that you bore all sin and its curse in your body, suffering the punishment for it all as You gave all Your blood as a ransom and cleansing. The water that symbolizes the Holy Spirit gives the same victorious testimony of all You did. I come through the curtain, our riven side, into holy and sweet fellowship with You, Lord Jesus.

ADDITIONAL SCRIPTURES TO CONSIDER

John 7:39; 15:26; 20:27;
Hebrews 12:24; Revelation 12:11

NOTES

JESUS' BLOOD

DAY 24

THE BLOOD SPEAKS

Leviticus 17:11 tells us that life is in the blood. A body can live without many of its parts—eyes, ears, legs, arms, hair—but it cannot live without blood. The blood in a body carries a message about the life of that body and also about its death.

The blood that came from Abel's body, for example, cried out for vengeance when his brother wrongfully killed him. (Hebrews 12:24)

However, even though Jesus, the perfect Lamb, was unjustly tortured and killed, His blood did not cry out for vengeance. Thank God! His blood was different from Abel's. Jesus' blood was proof of the punishment for our sin and the payment for our ransom. So Jesus' blood could legally cry out for mercy for us. God never had mercy on our sin. He judged it on Jesus. He legally gives us mercy because the awful death debt of our sin has been fully paid.

In the following verse, you see the contrast of the cry of Abel's blood that cried for vengeance and the blood of Jesus that speaks of mercy:

You have come to Jesus, the one who mediates the new covenant between God and people, and to the sprinkled blood, which speaks of forgiveness instead of crying out for vengeance like the blood of Abel (Hebrews 12:24 NLT).

COMMUNION

Precious Jesus, my Savior, as I take the bread and cup today, I am remembering and praising You for Your blood that speaks mercy for me because You received the punishment for my sin. I receive Your mercy and love.

ADDITIONAL SCRIPTURE TO CONSIDER

Genesis 4:10 NLT

NOTES

DAY 25

JESUS' BLOOD TESTIFIES

For there are three that testify: the Spirit, the water and the blood; and the three are in agreement.

1 John 5:7-8 NIV

The Spirit, the water (signifying Jesus' physical birth in a human body), and *the blood* are totally unified in their mighty testimony regarding us.

One definition that the dictionary gives to *testimony* is the statement or declaration of a witness under oath. A testimony is also considered evidence in support of a fact or statement. It is proof.

As we focus on the testimony of Jesus' blood, what fact does it support?

Think about it. Jesus bled as a result of God laying on Him the iniquity of us all. Jesus' blood testifies irrefutably of every detail that happened as a result of Him bearing our sin and sin's curse in His own body on the tree. The blood was there to witness, and now Jesus' blood is still speaking and giving testimony regarding what He took upon Himself for you.

Perhaps there is a lack of evidence of victory in your body or in an area of your life. You don't need to look to those areas for the evidence of victory when the blood supplies sufficient rock-solid proof that Jesus' work is complete for your whole person.

Sometimes there are symptoms and situations that appear as contrary evidence. This evidence can appear to define you and your circumstance. But the evidence the blood brings will change apparent contradictions because the blood was there and is the primary witness that Jesus overcame every contradiction.

COMMUNION

Precious Jesus, I take the bread and cup with a grateful and joyful heart today. Your blood is testifying about me. It is saying that everything wrong about me was put on You. You bled when You bore sin, sickness, dysfunction, weakness, and pain for me. Your blood is proof. It is indisputable evidence of what you accepted on my behalf. I refuse to bear what the blood says You bore on my behalf. I believe and agree with the testimony of the blood.

ADDITIONAL SCRIPTURES TO CONSIDER

1 John 5:6-8 NIV; Isaiah 53:5-6 NKJV

NOTES

DAY 26

AGREE WITH THE TESTIMONY OF THE BLOOD

And they have defeated him by the blood of the Lamb and by their testimony....

Revelation 12:11 NLT

What is *your* testimony going to be regarding your situation? You might have the thought, *Once the situation resolves, I will know then what the testimony is.* I'm not asking about your testimony in the future—it's your testimony today that counts. Right now. That's the one this verse is referring to. Are you going to testify about what you see with your eyes, hear with your ears, and what your feelings say? Or are you going to agree with the testimony of the blood? Did you know that you have a choice? And your choice of what you testify determines the outcome.

Second Corinthians 13:1 says that in the mouth of two or three witnesses every word is established.

Your testimony of agreement with what your senses say will confirm those things in your life. The testimony based on your senses when everything is going well doesn't pose a problem. It is when your testimony disagrees with the testimony of the blood that it becomes a problem. In essence, you'll end up bearing what He bore, and you don't have to do that! Agree with the blood.

Remember, you overcome by the agreement of these two vital testimonies: the blood of the Lamb *and* the word of *your testimony.*

COMMUNION

Lord Jesus, today as I commune with You over the bread and cup, I acknowledge the mighty testimony of Your blood about me. Your blood says that there was a perfect sacrifice on my behalf. Your blood is powerful proof that I am forgiven, healed, and redeemed from the enemy. Today, I overcome by the blood of the Lamb and my confirming testimony.

ADDITIONAL SCRIPTURES TO CONSIDER

Hebrews 12:24 NLT; 1 John 5:6-8 NLT;
Revelation 1:5 NLT

NOTES

THE PASSOVER

DAY 27

PASSOVER—THE LAMB

So the Egyptians worked the people of Israel without mercy. They made their lives bitter, forcing them to mix mortar and make bricks and do all the work in the fields. They were ruthless in all their demands.

Exodus 1:13-14 NLT

As a result of this life of slavery, the Israelites cried out for deliverance and God answered. On the last night of their captivity in Egypt, God instructed them to have a special meal that has become known as Passover. The meal was an entire roasted lamb without defect, salad of bitter greens, and unleavened bread. This family meal was to be eaten in the home, and there were to be no leftovers. (Exodus 12)

This would be an annual meal to remember the Israelites' supernatural exodus from Egypt. Eating the body of the Passover lamb was specifically for the health of each person eating. As the Israelites left Egypt, they all left healthy, according to this verse.

> *He also brought them out with silver and gold, and there was none feeble among His tribes* (Exodus 105:37 NKJV).

> *So the Lord led his people out from Egypt. They took with them valuable silver and gold things.* ***Nobody among the Israelite people was too weak to go*** (Psalm 105:37 EASY).

The lamb in this meal is also a picture of our perfect Jesus, sacrificed for our supernatural deliverance from the kingdom of darkness.

Jesus says, "Take eat. This is My body," about the bread, representing His body.

Paul warned that it is a lack of discerning or attention to the body of Christ that caused people in the church in Corinth to be weak, sickly, and even have premature death.

Humbly partaking, eating, of the sacrifice of Jesus' body heals us. Soul and body. Expect it.

One purpose Jesus' body was sacrificed was for our healing and deliverance.

COMMUNION

Jesus, precious Lamb of God, I acknowledge and worship You today. As I eat the bread that represents Your body, that bread will go into my body and become part of it, bringing healing and wholeness to every cell. As I eat and drink of the sacrificed Lamb, all weakness must go. I declare I am healed. I am whole. I am strong. I am delivered.

ADDITIONAL SCRIPTURES TO CONSIDER

John 1:29,36 NLT

NOTES

DAY 28

PASSOVER—THE BLOOD

Take special care of this chosen animal until the evening of the fourteenth day of this first month. Then the whole assembly of the community of Israel must slaughter their lamb or young goat at twilight. They are to take some of the blood and smear it on the sides and top of the doorframes of the houses where they eat the animal.

Exodus 12:6-7 NLT

The blood that represented and reflects the perfect life of the lamb was drained from its innocent body. That blood was then applied by a hyssop branch to the doorframe of the home of the family who was eating the lamb.

Every home with blood on its doorpost was protected from a death plague that came later that night. The blood of the little lamb had power to protect and save everyone in the house. Death passed over, not touching them.

COMMUNION

Blessed Lamb of God, I receive healing right now as I eat the bread that represents Your body that bore sickness, pain, and disease for me. I also drink the cup that represents Your blood that provides protection. I appropriate that protection today. The works of the enemy pass over me and my family, and ____________________. Thank You, Jesus, for the protection in Your blood. My heart rejoices to sing:

Oh the blood of Jesus
Oh the blood of Jesus
Oh the blood of Jesus
It keeps me safe and whole.

ADDITIONAL SCRIPTURE TO CONSIDER

Romans 3:25 NLT

NOTES

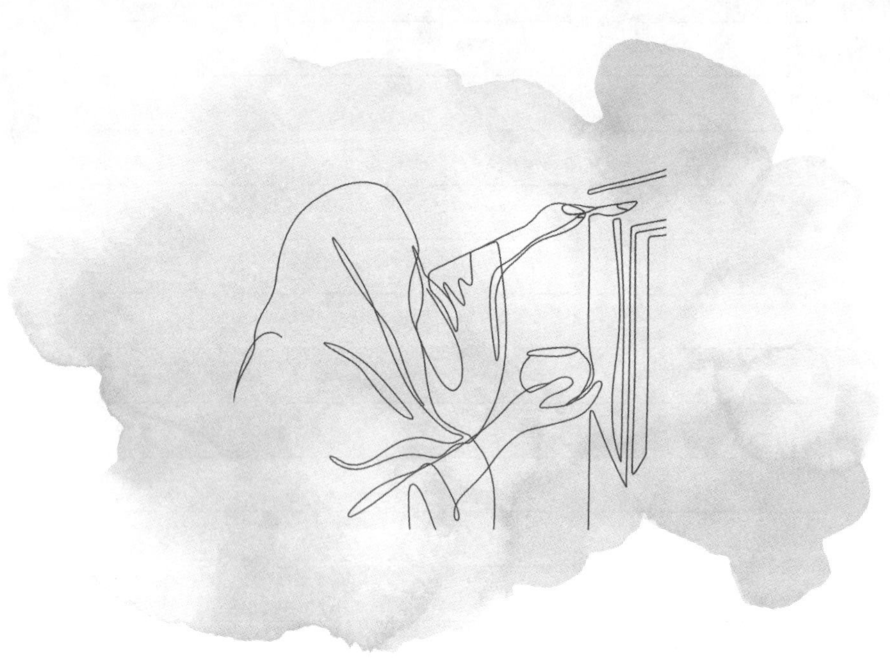

DAY 29

THE PASSOVER—THE APPLICATION

Drain the blood into a basin. Then take a bundle of hyssop branches and dip it into the blood. Brush the hyssop across the top and sides of the doorframes of your houses. And no one may go out through the door until morning. For the Lord will pass through the land to strike down the Egyptians. But when he sees the blood on the top and sides of the doorframe, the Lord will pass over your home. He will not permit his death angel to enter your house and strike you down.

Exodus 12:22-23 NLT

We know that the Passover lamb and its blood represents Jesus, our Lamb, and His blood. We understand that the body of the Lamb represents healing and strength to us and the blood is our protection and salvation. How is it that we apply the blood that Jesus shed to our lives, our home? What is our hyssop? The hyssop is our tongue. Our mouth. Say so! Our testimony. Saying what the body and blood of the Lamb are saying.

Eat the bread in trust in the Lamb. Drink the cup in faith in His powerful blood.

COMMUNION

Precious Lamb of God, today as I fellowship with You over the bread and cup, I thank You for my healing and health that You paid for by the scourging of Your body. I also purposefully apply Your wonder-working powerful blood by faith to my life and to my household for protection and all that salvation is. I apply the blood by saying the same thing it is saying about me. I overcome!

ADDITIONAL SCRIPTURES TO CONSIDER

Psalm 40:3 NLT; 89:1 NLT;
Matthew 21:16 NLT; Luke 6:45 NLT;
2 Corinthians 4:13 NLT

NOTES

WORTHY IS THE LAMB

DAY 30

THE LAMB ON THE THRONE

Together they will go to war against the Lamb, but the Lamb will defeat them because he is Lord of all lords and King of all kings. And his called and chosen and faithful ones will be with him.

Revelation 17:14 NLT

You would think that John the Revelator mixed up the Lamb and the Lion by mistake in this verse. Of course not! The might of the Lamb of God is apparently not fully realized.

There is much in the Bible referring to Jesus as the Lamb. The following is an overview:

- Once in the Old Testament (Isaiah 53:7)
- Twice in the Gospels (John 1:29,36)
- Once in Acts (Acts 8:32)
- Once in the Epistles (1 Peter 1:19)

- Twenty-six times in the book of Revelation

Eight of those 26 times, the throne is where the Lamb is.

Think about this. There will not be a single mark of sickness, sin, disease, or brokenness anywhere on our glorified bodies! The blessed body of the Lamb, however, will eternally bear the marks of what it cost Him to remove sin and the curse of sin from us. Simply looking at His hands and feet throughout eternity will always remind us of His great love.

Jesus' blood purchased an eternal redemption for us, and He will be eternally known as the Lamb.

COMMUNION

To the Lamb upon the throne, I bring my worship and gratefully remember the great work You accomplished. I praise You with all my heart today and forever that I am redeemed, not by gold or silver or by my good works—but by Your blood. You triumphed over my enemies and You are King of kings and Lord of lords.

ADDITIONAL SCRIPTURES TO CONSIDER

Revelation 5:6,13; 6:16; 7:9,10,17; 22:1,3 NLT;
John 20:20,27 NLT; Hebrews 9:12 NLT

NOTES

DAY 31

SONGS TO THE REDEEMER

*And they sang a new song with these words: "You are worthy to take the scroll and break its seals and open it. For you were slaughtered, and your blood has ransomed people for God from every tribe and language and people and nation. And you have caused them to become a Kingdom of priests for our God. And they will reign on the earth." Then I looked again, and I heard the voices of thousands and millions of angels around the throne and of the living beings and the elders. And they sang in a mighty chorus: "**Worthy is the Lamb who was slaughtered— to receive power and riches and wisdom and strength and honor and glory and blessing.**" And then I heard every creature in heaven and on earth and under the earth and in the sea. They sang: "Blessing and honor and glory and power belong to the one sitting on the throne **and to the Lamb forever and ever.**"*

Revelation 5:9-13 NLT

The scope of the impact of redemption's blood included and reached far beyond God's chosen people, Israel. The vast choir singing redemption's song around God's throne is made up of ransomed people from every tribe, language, ethnic group, and nation—making it incomparable to anything ever heard before.

Here on earth, from generation to generation, when the glorious story of the Cross and our redemption is known, people sing! The slaughter of Jesus' precious body and the pouring of His holy blood has brought us from death to life. From the kingdom of darkness to the kingdom of God's dear Son. There's much to sing about!

The redeemed who have already gone to heaven are already singing these gloriously joyful songs.

The angels and all the living beings and elders in heaven also pick up the melody of this song with the thrill and jubilation of what the blood testifies was accomplished.

> *And through him God reconciled everything to himself. He made peace with everything in heaven and on earth by means of Christ's blood on the cross* (Colossians 1:20 NLT).

COMMUNION

Dear Lord God, my heart is full of joy and I come with a song as I fellowship with You today over the bread and cup.

I will sing of my Redeemer,
And His wondrous love to me;
On the cruel cross He suffered,
From the curse to set me free.

Sing, oh, sing of my Redeemer,
With His blood He purchased me,
On the cross He sealed my pardon,
Paid the debt, and made me free.

I will praise my dear Redeemer,
His triumphant pow'r I'll tell,
How the victory He giveth
Over sin, and death, and hell.

I will sing of my Redeemer,
And His heav'nly love to me;
He from death to life hath brought me,
Son of God with Him to be.

"My Redeemer"
Philip Paul Bliss (1838-1876)
James McGranahan (1840-1907)

ADDITIONAL SCRIPTURES TO CONSIDER

Genesis 12:3 NLT; Mark 16:15 NLT

NOTES

EAT AGAIN AND AGAIN

That I may know Him *and the power of His resurrection, and the* ***fellowship of His sufferings,*** *being conformed to His death.*

Philippians 3:10 NKJV

FELLOWSHIP WITH JESUS AND HIS SUFFERINGS THROUGH COMMUNION

Paul yearned to know the fellowship of Jesus' sufferings in addition to knowing Him. What is the fellowship of His sufferings? There are meaningful interpretations of this scripture, all of which I acknowledge and appreciate.

But in this devotional we have been approaching this verse in the context of the Lord's Supper. At that table we fellowship with Him and the immense suffering that He undertook on our behalf.

We have come to this table for 31 days. These 31 days of fellowshipping with Jesus, purposefully using Communion to focus on and share His suffering, are finished. What now?

The invitation to continue to intimately commune with Him is ongoing. It is extended. The blessed Holy Spirit is always reaching out so that sweet fellowship with your Redeemer is never reduced to routine.

Here's what Jesus had to say about eating and drinking again and again and again. We find it in John 6, one of the most radically confronting chapters of Jesus' ministry.

At the beginning of the chapter, Jesus supernaturally feeds 5,000 men, plus women and children, and as a result, His popularity skyrocketed. By the end of the chapter, however, some people were offended and quit following Him. What happened in between that caused such a shift of popularity?

It all started with the subject of the miracle of multiplying bread, which they had been originally thrilled about. But then Jesus radically changed their focus when He said that *He* was the bread of life, that the Father had sent Him and that they should eat *Him.* If that wasn't bad enough, Jesus added that they should drink His blood too.

We have a great advantage in understanding the words of Jesus in this chapter because of His own explanation at the Last Supper. We also have the accounts from the Gospel writers about Jesus' passion and crucifixion. What Jesus said in John 6 about eating His flesh and drinking His blood is not confined to the Lord's Supper, but it obviously is included. Again, it's communion and fellowship that the Lord longs for us to share in with Him.

Before looking at particular verses in chapter 6, let's examine the very words that caused so much contention to better understand what Jesus was presenting to them. They are the words *eat* and *drink*.

There are two Greek words used repeatedly in the following passage that are both translated "eat." The first word, *phagēte,* in the most simple definition means to consume. The second Greek word translated as "eat" is *trōgōn.* This word carries the meaning of continuous action, again, in the most simple definition. It is even translated "to chew or gnaw." Can you picture that? The cultural and historical use of the Greek word most often used in these verses for "drink," *pinion,* pictured drinking as a daily activity.

With simple definitions of these Greek words, let's see how they are used by Jesus in the passage of scripture so we know what the people were hearing Jesus say.

> *So Jesus said again, "I tell you the truth, unless you eat* [phagēte] *the flesh of the Son of Man and drink* [piniōn] *his blood, you cannot have eternal life within you. But anyone who eats* [trōgōn] *my flesh and drinks* [piniōn] *my blood has eternal life, and I will raise that person at the last day. For my flesh is true food, and my blood is true drink. Anyone who eats* [trōgōn] *my flesh and drinks* [piniōn] *my blood remains in me, and I in him. I live because of the living Father who sent me; in the same way, anyone*

> *who feeds* [trōgōn] *on me will live because of me*" (John 6:53-57 NLT).

The first word for "eat," *phagēte,* has the meaning of a one-time event. The food is consumed. I believe that even if we don't realize it, we partake of Jesus and His work on the Cross when we are born again. That particular "eat" doesn't need to be repeated. Once you are born again, there is no need for that supernatural rebirth to be repeated.

However, being born again is not the last time we partake of Jesus. The second word for "eat," *trōgōn,* denotes *continuous action.* Jesus says we are to do that. *Not gulping it down quickly, but chewing, gnawing.* Imagining that action is quite confronting actually, and for the people Jesus was talking to in John 6, it was extremely revolting to them because it sounded like cannibalism.

Jesus was talking about eating a spiritual meal, however, and absolutely not eating His physical body and drinking His physical blood. The meaning of this word *trōgōn* reminds me of the Hebrew word for meditate, *hagah,* in Joshua 1:8, which means "to murmur, to ponder, to speak, to utter, to think about it, to picture it, to internalize it; as a cow chews and rechews the nutrients out of its food."

Based upon this very clear instruction from Jesus as well as direction to continue to eat the bread and drink the cup till He comes again, you can be certain that Communion is to be repeated.

The benefits of daily, repeated spiritual eating and drinking are enormous. What spiritual nutrient is in the truly super food of Jesus' body and blood? Eternal life.

I have surely experienced the Holy Spirit's patient encouragement to repeat and look again at the same detail of Jesus' suffering until I finally really understood what He meant for me to see, experience, and realize about a vital union with Jesus.

If I would have just taken Communion in the same frame of mind, with the same habitual approach, I would have missed the priceless impact of what He did 2,000 years ago to an area of my life now. I would have come short of a better understanding of His substitutionary work.

The Father wants the suffering and work of the Lamb of God to affect your entire life on a daily basis. Be ready for the Holy Spirit to move your awareness of the details of Jesus' suffering from an annual, monthly, or even weekly event to a daily fellowship.

Would being so aware of Jesus' suffering make you sad and depressed? No! The opposite will happen. Jesus' suffering wasn't for nothing. Each detail of suffering on His body released the blood that brought redemption and victory to each area of your life!

As a result of this, your gratefulness, love, and depth of worship to Him will increase more and more. Cliches regarding His great work will melt away and each word of praise will carry great meaning.

FRESH VERSUS LEFTOVERS

There are no definite instructions regarding how often you are to take Communion. But like prayer, you will have to guard it from becoming a ritual. The same instruction that Jesus gave to the woman at the well in John 4 regarding worship applies to Communion.

> *God is Spirit, and those who worship Him must worship in spirit and truth* (John 4:24 NKJV).

Words that are said over and over have the potential of drifting from something heartfelt to something we can say while we are forming a to-do list for the day. What can we do to keep our fellowship real and fresh as we repeat the Lord's Supper? Let the Holy Spirit help you. Look to Him to teach and remind you of the truth. This helps to keep your heart engaged consciously of the Lord.

Asking and earnestly yearning to know Jesus more like Paul did in Philippians 3:8-10, communicates not only a sacred admiration of the Lord but a humble admission that you don't know everything there is to know about Him. Is there more for you to know? Ask.

God loves to reveal Himself, and the Bible gives accounts of these revelations to many characters in the Old and New Testaments. Some of those revelations of Himself were quite bold. Like when He spoke to Moses on the back side of the desert (Exodus 3), or when Jesus confronted and introduced Himself to Saul on the road to Damascus (Acts 9). More often, the Lord comes less dramatically and as John describes in Revelation:

> *Here I am! I stand at the door and knock. If anyone hears my voice and opens the door, I will come in and eat with that person, and they with me* (Revelation 3:20 NIV).

Obviously, this kind of interaction with the Lord will go no further, unless you really want it to. You have to open the door. But when you do, wow! He promises to come in and share a meal with you. He shares on more topics than Communion, of course. However, your response to His ongoing invitation, His knocking on your heart's door, includes His invitation to eat the bread and drink the cup, opening your heart to Him.

Jesus is definitely desiring that His interaction with you is more than a cold religious ritual and is inviting and encouraging daily communion and intimate fellowship with Him. For those of us who love and follow Jesus, this invitation to eat and drink of our Lord again and again is not offensive. Instead, it is an honor and something to definitely take Jesus up on.

It is my prayer that the 31 days of this devotional interrupted what may have been a routine approach to communion and that a beautiful possibility of knowing Jesus more was introduced. I pray that you have a stirring of holy curiosity to know more specifically about aspects of Jesus' body, His precious blood and suffering on your behalf.

NOTES

EPILOGUE

Early on Saturday morning, September 6, 2025, Patsy Cameneti's place of residence changed, and she moved on to heaven. After a few years of some significant health challenges, Patsy chose to go home to see the Savior she loved and served all her life.

At every stage and in each phase of treatment and recovery, she stood in absolute faith and victory. The healing power of God rescued her more than once along this journey.

Patsy experienced God's mighty quickening power in a very real and obvious way, especially as she continued to minister the Word. She pressed on in ministry by the strength of God.

Patsy fulfilled the number of her days in victory, and she chose the better part. These verses were particularly meaningful to her.

> *For I know that this will turn out for my deliverance through your prayer and the supply of the Spirit of*

Jesus Christ, according to my earnest expectation and hope that in nothing I shall be ashamed, but with all boldness, as always, so now also Christ will be magnified in my body, whether by life or by death. For to me, to live is Christ, and to die is gain. But if I live on in the flesh, this will mean fruit from my labor; yet what I shall choose I cannot tell. For I am hard-pressed between the two, having a desire to depart and be with Christ, which is far better (Philippians 1:19–23 NKJV).

And when this perishable puts on the imperishable and this that was capable of dying puts on freedom from death, then shall be fulfilled the Scripture that says, Death is swallowed up (utterly vanquished forever) in and unto victory (1 Corinthians 15:54 AMPC).

Jenny Eddison

Ministry Assistant, Prayer Partner, and Friend

Patsy Cameneti was born in the mountain town of Salida, Colorado. She grew up as the daughter of Pentecostal pastors in the farmlands of Colorado. Her parents, Bill and Ginger Behrman, pioneered and pastored Assembly of God churches in Castle Rock and Burlington, Colorado.

As Patsy Behrman, she graduated from Rhema Bible Training Center in 1977 and then worked at Kenneth Hagin

Ministries and Rhema Bible Training Center for 16 years as vocal director of Faith's Creation, the All Faiths Crusades, the Director of the Prayer and Healing Center, and as an instructor at Rhema Bible Training Center.

Patsy was always compelled to help believers find their place in Christ. Her message, which often emphasized prayer, is marked by a personal pursuit of God that has inspired many believers to also develop their own walk with God in a real and purposeful way.

For more than 40 years, she and her husband, Tony, have taught and preached about the goodness of God and mankind's total redemption accomplished through Jesus. Their desire has always been to equip the body of Christ with biblical tools to fulfill God's plans and purpose.

They founded Bible schools in Australia and Papua New Guinea, and also established an orphanage in Kathmandu, Nepal.

Patsy served with her husband Tony as foundation pastors of Rhema Family Church—a vibrant, multi-ethnic church in the suburbs of Brisbane.

Every year, Patsy traveled worldwide speaking to a wide range of peoples and groups. Her voice and influence have impacted many people and will continue to do so.

Equipping Believers to Walk in the Abundant Life

John 10:10b

Connect with us for fresh content and news about forthcoming books from your favorite authors...

In the Right Hands, This Book Will Change Lives!

Most of the people who need this message will not be looking for this book. To change their lives, you need to **put a copy of this book in their hands.**

Our ministry is constantly seeking methods to find the people who need this anointed message to change their lives. **Will you help us reach these people?**

From

Patsy Camaneti

Work in a Divine Partnership with God to Unleash Power in Your Prayers

Are you longing for a deeper, more effective prayer life? Do you want to pray with more accuracy and precision? God never meant for you to do this alone! You are meant to co-labor with Almighty God, tapping into the unlimited resources of heaven.

Patsy Cameneti, a global leader on the topic of prayer, invites you to pray from a position of victory, accessing God's presence, power, and provision. She offers fresh insight on how to escape the snare of praying solely from earthly knowledge and learning to engage in Spirit-led prayer, hindered by nothing.

With practical tools and revelation, you will learn how to:

- Break free from earth-bound prayers and ascend to a realm where God's plans are revealed
- Shift from praying to convince God to do something to prayers empowered by what God already wills
- Recognize God's Word as a powerful weapon in your spiritual arsenal
- Partner with Jesus as the stairway between heaven and earth, revealing God's purposes for every prayer you utter

Embrace scripture, prophecy, and praise as access points into the spirit realm and become a force against the enemy! God has called you to a higher place of prayer—a partnership with Him. It's time to align your prayers with heaven's perspective, tapping into resources that can only be found in the spirit realm.

Purchase your copy wherever books are sold

From

Patsy Cameneti

What was God thinking when He ***ENGENDERED*** or created male and female? What does that have to do with gender roles? And is that purpose still relevant today?

Patsy Cameneti boldly explores God's thoughts and creative intention for humankind. Stripping away cultural and traditional thinking, she examines raw truths from God's Word about gender, sexuality, marriage, and family that deliver practical insights into your everyday life. *Engendered* doesn't shy away from topics of the day and brings God's perspective to subjects like these:

- How to enjoy marriage as God designed it
- What God thinks about sex
- Sexuality and gender clarity
- Representing God in the way you parent
- Reflecting God's image through gender roles

As you discover God's original purpose and design for these areas, you'll be enlightened and empowered to live the life God ***ENGENDERED*** for you from the beginning.

Purchase your copy wherever books are sold